EXPLORING COUNTRIES
Indonesia

by Lisa Owings

BLASTOFF! READERS
5

BELLWETHER MEDIA • MINNEAPOLIS, MN

Note to Librarians, Teachers, and Parents:

Blastoff! Readers are carefully developed by literacy experts and combine standards-based content with developmentally appropriate text.

Level 1 provides the most support through repetition of high-frequency words, light text, predictable sentence patterns, and strong visual support.

Level 2 offers early readers a bit more challenge through varied simple sentences, increased text load, and less repetition of high-frequency words.

Level 3 advances early-fluent readers toward fluency through increased text and concept load, less reliance on visuals, longer sentences, and more literary language.

Level 4 builds reading stamina by providing more text per page, increased use of punctuation, greater variation in sentence patterns, and increasingly challenging vocabulary.

Level 5 encourages children to move from "learning to read" to "reading to learn" by providing even more text, varied writing styles, and less familiar topics.

Whichever book is right for your reader, Blastoff! Readers are the perfect books to build confidence and encourage a love of reading that will last a lifetime!

This edition first published in 2013 by Bellwether Media, Inc.

No part of this publication may be reproduced in whole or in part without written permission of the publisher. For information regarding permission, write to Bellwether Media, Inc., Attention: Permissions Department, 5357 Penn Avenue South, Minneapolis, MN 55419.

Library of Congress Cataloging-in-Publication Data
Owings, Lisa.
Indonesia / by Lisa Owings.
     p. cm. – (Blastoff! readers. Exploring countries)
Includes bibliographical references and index.
Summary: "Developed by literacy experts for students in grades three through seven, this book introduces young readers to the geography and culture of Indonesia"–Provided by publisher.
ISBN 978-1-60014-763-0 (hardcover : alk. paper)
 1. Indonesia–Juvenile literature. I. Title. II. Series: Blastoff! readers. 5, Exploring countries.
DS615.O95 2013
959.8–dc23   2012007667

Printed in the United States of America, North Mankato, MN.

Contents

N
W E
S

Philippines

Malaysia

Indian
Ocean

Jakarta

Indonesia

East Timor

Did you know?

Indonesia includes parts of
New Guinea and Borneo. These
are the second and third largest
islands in the world.

Australia

Pacific
Ocean

Papua
New Guinea

Indonesia is an **archipelago** made
up of more than 17,500 islands.
These islands and their surrounding
waters stretch over 735,358 square
miles (1,904,569 square kilometers).
This makes Indonesia the largest
country in Southeast Asia.

Indonesia lies between the Indian
and Pacific Oceans. Malaysia and
the Philippines are its neighbors to
the north. Papua New Guinea shares
a border in the east. Australia lies
to the southeast. The tiny country
of East Timor occupies the same
island as Indonesia's West Timor.

Indonesia's largest islands
are Sumatra, Java, Kalimantan,
Sulawesi, and Papua. The
crowded island of Java holds
the nation's capital, Jakarta.

The **tropical** islands of Indonesia are spread out along the **equator**. This means the weather is warm and damp in most areas. The land stays lush and green all year. Indonesia's wet season is marked by **monsoons**. These storms bring heavy rains from December to March.

Volcanoes rise in the centers of the larger islands. Mosses, oaks, and tea grow in the cool mists of the high mountains. **Rain forests** cover the lower hills and spread toward the islands' edges. The coastal areas are low and muddy. Some islands have **mangrove** forests or white-sand beaches.

mangrove forest

Mount Merapi

Did you know?

When Krakatoa erupted, it spewed ash 50 miles (80 kilometers) into the air. The ash blocked out the sun for days. It also caused deep red sunsets for months afterward.

Indonesia has more active volcanoes than any other country in the world. Their ash makes the soil rich and **fertile**. However, volcanoes can also be destructive. Java's Mount Merapi is the deadliest of Indonesia's more than 100 active volcanoes. Its **eruptions** in 2010 killed more than 300 people. Thousands were forced to abandon their homes.

Krakatoa is the most famous volcano in Indonesia. Its eruption in 1883 was one of the most violent in history. The volcano blew itself apart in an explosion that could be heard 2,200 miles (3,500 kilometers) away. This produced **tsunamis** that destroyed nearly everything around Krakatoa.

fun fact

Three lakes of different colors fill the Mount Kelimutu volcano. Locals believe one lake holds young souls, another holds elderly souls, and the last holds evil souls.

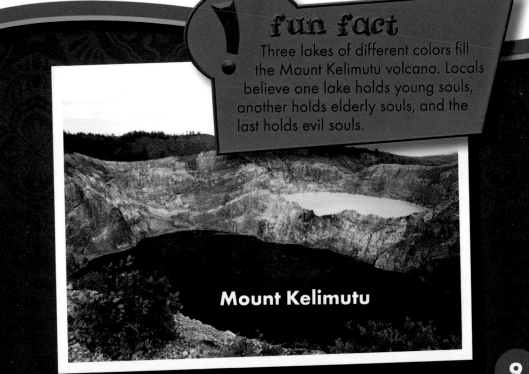

Mount Kelimutu

babirusa

proboscis monkeys

monster flower

fun fact
The world's largest flower blooms in Indonesia. The monster flower weighs up to 24 pounds (11 kilograms) and smells like rotting meat.

Indonesia's placement between Asia and Australia makes it home to animals from both continents. A few rhinoceroses, elephants, and tigers survive in the forests of the western islands. Scaly pangolins hide from leopards and other predators on Sumatra.

Komodo dragons can only be found in Indonesia. These giant lizards weigh around 300 pounds (135 kilograms) and kill large prey with their venomous bite.

Komodo dragon

Orangutans and proboscis monkeys swing through the trees of Kalimantan forests. Cockatoos, butterflies, and birds of paradise fly over the eastern islands. Papua is home to fuzzy tree kangaroos. Babirusas also live in the east. These wild pigs have tusks that grow through their noses. Sea turtles and brightly colored fish swim in **coral reefs** offshore.

Indonesia has the fourth largest population in the world. More than 248 million people are scattered across about 6,000 islands. They represent more than 300 cultures, speak more than 600 languages, and follow several religions. About four out of every ten Indonesians are Javanese. Most Javanese live on Java, are Muslim, and speak Javanese. The Sundanese are the next largest group. Smaller numbers of Madurese, Balinese, Chinese, and many other peoples add to Indonesia's **diversity**.

Indonesians also have much in common. They are known for being friendly, artistic, and spiritual. They also share the country's official language, Bahasa Indonesia. This common language helps Indonesians learn about and celebrate one another's differences.

Speak Bahasa Indonesia!

Bahasa Indonesia means "the language of Indonesia."

English	Indonesian	How to say it
hello	halo	HAH-loh
good-bye	selamat tinggal	suh-LAH-MAHT TING-gahl
yes	ya	YAH
no	tidak	tee-DAH
please	tolong	TOH-lohng
thank you	terima kasih	tuh-REE-mah KAH-see
friend	teman	tuh-MAHN

fun fact

Many Indonesian men and women wear *sarongs*. These rectangles of colorful fabric are usually wrapped around the waist like a skirt.

More than half of Indonesians live in the countryside. Their wooden houses are often built on tall posts to protect them from floodwaters. Most people use boats, bicycles, motorcycles, or their feet to get to the local market. Groups farthest from large cities have little to no contact with the modern world.

More Indonesians move to cities every year. They live in modern apartments or houses and take cars, buses, or trains to work. Locals and **tourists** catch rides on three-wheeled taxis called *bajaj*. Religion is a large part of daily life throughout the country. Most Indonesians are Muslim. They pray five times a day.

Where People Live in Indonesia

cities
44%

countryside
56%

Did you know?

Bali is the only Indonesian island where most people are Hindu or Buddhist. Balinese religious ceremonies attract many tourists to the island.

Most Indonesian children attend elementary
school between ages 6 and 12. They study
art, math, science, social studies, and religion.
Every student learns Bahasa Indonesia.
Most also study English.

Secondary school is divided into three years of middle school and three years of high school. Only about half of Indonesian students go on to middle school. Even fewer finish high school. Many leave school so they can help their families earn money. Those who do finish high school can choose to attend a university in Indonesia or study **abroad**.

Working

Did you know?
Indonesia is known for its artistic fabric. *Batik* is made by painting designs on a cloth with wax. Then the fabric is dipped in dye.

Where People Work in Indonesia

- manufacturing 13%
- farming 38%
- services 49%

Farmers grow a variety of crops in Indonesia's fertile countryside. Rice is the main crop on Java. Large farms on Sumatra grow coffee beans, tea, and cocoa beans to sell to other countries. Rubber, palm oil, and spices are also harvested in Sumatra. The forests of Kalimantan and Papua provide teak and other rare woods. Fish and shrimp are caught in the ocean or raised in ponds.

Factories in cities process the country's oil, natural gas, and coal. Indonesia is also rich in tin, copper, and gold. Many workers on Bali and Java work at hotels and restaurants. They serve the millions of tourists that visit each year.

Did you know?

Young men on the island of Nias have a unique way of proving their strength. They jump over a stone wall that stands 6 feet (2 meters) tall.

Indonesians enjoy playing and watching sports. **Badminton** and soccer are favorites. *Sepak takraw* is popular in the countryside. It is similar to volleyball, but players keep the ball in the air with their feet. Many people practice an Indonesian **martial art** called *pencak silat*. Girls often learn the **traditional** dance of their region.

Families swim, surf, or fly kites at the beach. They also explore the country's mountains and forests. People sometimes visit nearby tourist attractions such as Komodo Island or Borobudur Temple. Indonesians also enjoy watching television, going to movies, and playing chess.

fun fact

The annual bull races held on Madura are always exciting. Participants feed their bulls eggs, honey, and chili peppers to give them strength. During the race, riders steer from a wooden sled between the bulls.

Rice is a **staple** in Indonesia. People eat it plain, with coconut milk, or flavored with spices. Rice is usually sticky because Indonesians prefer to eat with their fingers.

Gado-gado is a Javanese specialty of vegetables, egg, and tofu with peanut sauce. Roast pig, or *babi guling*, is the most famous Balinese dish. People on Kalimantan and Sulawesi enjoy grilled fish. *Satay* carts throughout the country offer skewers of roasted meat. Indonesians often enjoy tropical fruits for dessert.

gado-gado

satay

fun fact

Durian fruits are large and spiky. They taste creamy and sweet, but they are so stinky that many public places have banned them.

23

Did you know?

On Independence Day, prizes sit atop tall poles that are coated in grease. People work together to reach the top by climbing on one another's shoulders.

Nyepi

Nearly all holidays in Indonesia are religious. The biggest Islamic holiday is *Lebaran*, a celebration of the end of **Ramadan**. Muslim families gather to pray, feast on traditional foods, and ask one another to forgive past mistakes.

Waisak is a Buddhist holiday that celebrates the birth, life, and death of Buddha. Buddhists gather at the Borobudur Temple to pray and give offerings of flowers and fruit. Christians celebrate Christmas and Easter. Many Indonesians mark Independence Day on August 17 with races and other fun contests.

fun fact

The instruments in a gamelan orchestra are thought to contain powerful spirits. Gamelan players consider it disrespectful to touch the instruments with their feet or step over them.

Drama and dance are closely linked in Indonesian culture. *Wayang* is an ancient form of Indonesian drama. Carefully crafted puppets are used to tell Hindu stories. Their shadows are cast on a screen lit from behind. A **gamelan orchestra** provides music.

The most famous Indonesian forms of dance are Balinese and Javanese. Both styles feature dancers with elaborate costumes. Balinese dancers tell stories with hand gestures, wide eyes, and quick movements. Javanese dances are slower and quieter. Indonesians of all backgrounds use drama and dance to show pride in their culture.

Balinese dancers

Fast Facts About Indonesia

Indonesia's flag

Indonesia's flag has a simple design that dates back to the 1200s. The top half is red, and the bottom half is white. The red stands for courage. White represents honesty and purity. This flag was officially adopted four years before Indonesia gained independence from the Netherlands in 1949.

Official Name: Republic of Indonesia

Area: 735,358 square miles (1,904,569 square kilometers); Indonesia is the 15th largest country in the world.

Capital City:	Jakarta
Important Cities:	Surabaya, Bandung, Medan, Semarang
Population:	248,216,193 (July 2012)
Official Language:	Bahasa Indonesia
National Holiday:	Independence Day (August 17)
Religions:	Muslim (86.1%), Christian (8.7%), Other (3.4%), Hindu (1.8%)
Major Industries:	farming, fuel, manufacturing, mining, services, tourism
Natural Resources:	oil, natural gas, coal, tin, copper, gold, silver, wood, farmland
Manufactured Products:	fuel, clothing, cement, plywood, rubber, food products
Farm Products:	rice, cassava, peanuts, palm oil, cocoa beans, coffee beans, tea, poultry, beef, pork, eggs
Unit of Money:	Indonesian rupiah

Glossary

abroad—outside of one's home country

archipelago—a group of islands

badminton—a game played with racquets, a high net, and a small shuttlecock; players hit the shuttlecock back and forth over the net.

coral reefs—underwater structures made of coral; reefs usually grow in shallow seawater.

diversity—inclusion of people from different backgrounds or cultures

equator—an imaginary line around the center of the earth; the equator divides the planet into a northern half and a southern half.

eruptions—events in which a volcano shoots out lava, hot ash, and steam

fertile—able to support growth

gamelan orchestra—an Indonesian musical group that plays mostly metal instruments; gamelan orchestras traditionally play during dramatic performances, dances, and religious ceremonies.

mangrove—a type of tree that grows in shallow saltwater and is propped up by its roots

martial art—a style of fighting or self-defense; kung fu, tae kwon do, and jujitsu are types of martial arts.

monsoons—large storms with very strong winds

rain forests—dense tropical forests where rain falls most of the year

Ramadan—the ninth month of the Islamic calendar; Ramadan is a time when Muslims do not eat from sunrise to sunset.

staple—a product that is widely and regularly used

tourists—people who are visiting a country

traditional—relating to stories, beliefs, or ways of life that families or groups hand down from one generation to the next

tropical—part of the tropics; the tropics is a hot, rainy region around the equator.

tsunamis—powerful waves that are sometimes caused by volcanic eruptions

To Learn More

AT THE LIBRARY
Gelman, Rita Golden. *Rice Is Life*. New York, N.Y.: Henry Holt & Company, 2000.

Owings, Lisa. *The Komodo Dragon*. Minneapolis, Minn.: Bellwether Media, 2012.

Zimmerman, Dwight Jon. *The Day the World Exploded: The Earthshaking Catastrophe at Krakatoa*. New York, N.Y.: Collins, 2007.

ON THE WEB
Learning more about Indonesia is as easy as 1, 2, 3.

1. Go to www.factsurfer.com.

2. Enter "Indonesia" into the search box.

3. Click the "Surf" button and you will see a list of related Web sites.

With factsurfer.com, finding more information is just a click away.

Index